MILLION DOLLAR AFFAIR

A Self-Help Guide to
Personal Growth
While Building
a 7-Figure Business

EVAN-NICOLE WILLIAMS

Madison + Park
A Global Branding Agency

Copyright © 2024 Evan-Nicole Williams
Written by Evan-Nicole Williams

Published by Madison + Park
Cover Photography by Hassan Richardson

All rights reserved. No part of this book may be reproduced, stored, or transmitted by any means—whether auditory, graphic, mechanical, or electronic—without written permission of both publisher and author, except in the case of brief excerpts used in critical articles and reviews. Unauthorized reproduction of any part of this work is illegal and is punishable by law.

978-1-7346316-8-5 (Hardcover)
978-1-7346316-9-2 (Softcover)

Because of the dynamic nature of the internet, any web addresses or links contained in this book may have changed since publication and may no longer be valid. The views expressed in this work are solely those of the author and do not necessarily reflect the views of the publisher, and the publisher hereby disclaims any responsibility for them.

Published 2024

United States of America

To my grandparents:
Joan, John, Mary, Roosevelt

Thank you for loving me and always making me feel so special.
I owe you everything and I hope that you are proud.
Without you, there is no me, so thank you.
I love you so much.

With Love & Gratitude,

Your granddaughter

"Ebbie Cole"

A Letter to my Paw Paw,

A life without you, I never imagined. The news still hangs heavy in the air. You, a Leo in all his fiery glory, raised five roaring flames of your own, and together with Grandma, you built a family that stretched its warmth across four generations, me included. I can still hear your infectious laugh, a melody forever intertwined with your gruff jokes and twinkling eyes. 80 years, a life rich and full, a heart that overflowed with the warmth of a thousand suns. Gone, they say, but how can the sun truly set when its light has touched so many lives?

27th of December, the date carved itself into my heart, a marker of an ending and a poignant beginning. This book, with its whispers of love and loss, is a tribute to that beginning, a testament to the fire you ignited within me. You weren't just a grandfather, you were a confidante, a storyteller, a champion. Now, as I embark on this new chapter, a "Million Dollar Affair" of my own, your absence is a constant ache. But your spirit, Paw Paw, burns bright within me. Your lessons whisper in my ear, your laughter fuels my courage, your love a compass guiding me through uncharted waters.

This Million Dollar Affair may be about wealth and power, but the true riches, I know now, lie in the connections we forge, the love we share, the legacies we leave behind. And your legacy, Paw Paw, is a treasure beyond measure. It's the echo of your laughter, the warmth of your hugs, the strength of your spirit. It's the love that binds us, a love that even death cannot sever.

So, this book, this journey, I dedicate it to you, my Leo, my guiding light. May your story live on in these pages, an inspiration to all who seek, love, and dream.

With love that transcends time and space,

Your legacy will forever live through me.

Sincerely,

A Williams Girl

Contents

Foreword   vii

Introduction   1

Luke 12:48   5

The Million Dollar Dream   11

Million Dollar Mindset: Overcoming Challenges   19

The Million Dollar Journey   27

Building the Million Dollar Team   37

Million Dollar Marketing Guru   43

The Power of Networking   53

Million Dollar Balance: Business vs. Personal   59

Defining Your Success: The Art of Becoming   67

God's Plan: The Million Dollar Celebration & Building a Legacy   75

Afterword   87

Foreword

By Sherita Cherry-Williams (Mom)

To My Beloved Daughter,

As I stand on the threshold of introducing this remarkable book to the world, I find myself overcome with a profound sense of pride and gratitude. From the moment you were placed in my arms as a tiny, delicate bundle, the doctor walked into the room and asked were we your parents? We looked astounded when we said, "Is she ok?" He said that our little girl was something "special." Those words echoed in my heart, and today, as I reflect on the incredible journey that has unfolded since then, those words ring truer than ever.

I have had the unparalleled privilege of watching you grow from a sweet, giggling baby to the incredible young woman you are today. As your parent, I have witnessed the unfolding of your character, the development of your Christian faith, and the unwavering love that emanates from your very being. Your journey has been a testament to resilience, faith, and a spirit that radiates kindness and compassion.

From childhood to pre-teen, it was evident that you were destined for something extraordinary at a young age. As your parent, I took on the intentional role of guardian, nurturing your growth and safeguarding the flame of your potential. Today, as you present the world with this book, it is a culmination of your Christian faith, your desire to uplift others, and the love that you so freely give.

You are uniquely qualified to pen these pages because you don't just talk the talk; you walk the walk. Your life is a living example of our principles and values. From teaching you the importance of being your own cheerleader to emphasizing the value of self-love, how to move in silence, and finding strength through prayer and trust in God, your wisdom has not only been spoken but demonstrated in the daily tapestry of your existence.

In the face of adversities, you demonstrated a strength that is beyond your years, a testament to the character you were shaping. I watched you confront challenges head-on, staying true to your convictions and emerging not just unscathed but strengthened by the experiences. Your ability to stay focused and accountable for your actions has been nothing short of inspiring, which gives you confidence that this book will change the lives of many.

You were positioned to win, not by chance, but by design. From the earliest days, you were set up to conquer the challenges that life would present. Your journey has been a training ground, shaping you into a person of strength, resilience, and fierceness. Your story is not just one of personal triumph; it is a beacon of inspiration for all who dare to dream, aspire, and believe.

In the pages of this book, you generously share the insights gained from your own experiences, baring your soul with transparency to guide others on their journey. Your words are not just motivational; they are a call to action, an invitation for readers to embrace the process, trust in their unique positioning, and unapologetically pursue their goals.

As your parent, it is with overwhelming pride and love that I commend this book to the world. May it resonate with the hearts of many, inspiring them to embrace their own journeys with faith, courage, and a resolute belief that they too, are positioned to win.

So proud of you!

With love,

Mommy
Sherita Cherry-Williams

January 24, 2023

Journal Entry:

"We are currently at 70.3k in sales for Glam Affair Hair Co. in the month of January! What a way to kick off the year Guru! This has never happened! I am so proud of my small but BIG business! I went from making 6 figures in a year to 6 figures in a month! BUT GOD! I serve a BIG GOD!!!

100k sales/month 1,000,000/year! I claim it in 2023!

No help, no handouts! God, I trust you.

Thank You in advance for all you do for me; my creatives, the strategy, God, you know my heart & I am so thankful I know You!

I am proud of myself today.

xoxo,

Guru

INTRODUCTION

I would love to start this book by telling you how much of an amazing person I am, how life is so easy, nothing bothers me, and how fun it is to make a Million Dollars every night in your sleep, buttttttt if we're going to be anything, let's BE FOR REAL. I actually want the opening of this book to be as raw and honest as possible. As I am writing this, I am currently still on the journey to making my First Million Dollars in sales for my hair company, Glam Affair Hair Co., but as you are reading this, know that Glam Affair Hair Co. has now hit a Million Dollars in Sales and I am now, a proud "business mom."

Woman to woman, I want to first thank you for choosing YOU! For you to be reading this right now, I know that there is something in you longing for something you have never experienced, whether it is a dream that you've been holding onto for many years or a desire of your heart that has yet to unfold, I want you to know that on the other side of this journey is everything you never knew you needed. You can see it now; Life is peaceful. Joy is your best friend, and everything you want wants you back.

I would be lying if I said this journey isn't going to be rough! This book is simply NOT for the weak-hearted. As I pour my heart into these pages, I pray that you fight to find as much clarity in your human experience as I am working diligently to do in mine. Nothing worth having comes easy, including the success you are working so hard to achieve. Every day will not be the same day, but every day, we have another chance to grow, evolve, and become our best selves.

A part of me hesitated as I began to write this book because I wasn't sure how vulnerable I could really be or how much of myself I wanted to pour. Still, I knew and reminded myself daily that there was a woman somewhere in this world who needed me and needed an extra push into greatness. I've endured a lot as I've climbed this ladder, and I am still not where I want to be every second of every day, but I now understand what it requires and how much of me has to show up in the season of "becoming." Some days are more challenging than others, but I am strong enough. YOU ARE STRONG ENOUGH.

This book will be a tool of guidance for the woman daring to dream both BIG and BOLD. This book will serve as the missing piece that I wish I had as I traveled into the long, painful, but rewarding journey of success and womanhood. As you both read and reflect, please share your thoughts on the lines provided to help you navigate and come back to as a reference as you grow. I am here to pour all of my love and light into you on your quest to discovering and becoming. I am here to help you make your next move, a MILLION DOLLAR ONE!

CHAPTER

LUKE 12:48

"To whom much is given, much is required."

I would like for you to read that over and over again. I want you to focus on one word and one word only: "REQUIRED." I'm sure we have all heard this biblical phrase over and over again, and for some reason, it hit it on the nail for me every time. Check out the definition of the word *required* below.

REQUIRED.

/rəˈkwī(ə)rd/

ADJECTIVE

1. essential, needed, or necessary

We all know that God has blessed us with so much. He has given us all unique talents, resources, and spiritual gifts according to His will for our lives so that He may be glorified. There is nothing ABOUT you that God does not already know. There is nothing IN you that God didn't fearfully and wonderfully placed. You are exactly who He has called you to be, and He has equipped you with everything you need to be fruitful and multiply.

Knowing that God has blessed and continues to bless me in the simplest of ways reassures me that I am always at the right place at the right time in this journey. Whether you are in the beauty industry, the music industry, the medical field, an entrepreneur, or even working your way up the corporate ladder, God has placed in you something so special that no one can ever take from you, and that is your heart, your mind, and your gifts.

The first step to knowing what is required of you on your journey to becoming the best version of yourself is KNOWING what God placed in you. Are you aware of your gifts and your talents? What are some of the things that make you unique? What sets you apart from everyone else around you? Do you know?

Take a moment to honestly think and write down some of the amazing gifts and talents that you have below:

_____
_____
_____
_____
_____

I also want you to write down all of the things that you believe in God for in this next season of your life. Be open and honest, and no matter how BIG or small the dream/desire is, WRITE IT DOWN.

When we set our intentions on asking God for the desires of our heart, I don't think that we always understand what comes with it. It is so easy to ask God for a million dollars. It is so easy to ask God for a new car, a new house, a better relationship, or a better job, but do we really know what is required of us to have those things? It takes WORK. Like I said before, *something worth having takes work.*

God will always require MORE from you in order to align with the desires of your heart without losing sight of the one who gave it to you. There is no way to achieve better outcomes than to strive for better in every way possible. In order to get GREAT results, you must put in GREAT work. In order to get MEDIOCRE results, all you need is MEDIOCRE work. This is law.

Imagine becoming a Millionaire. Imagine having a successful business, purchasing that new fancy car or a new home for your family. Imagine having your dream body or meeting the love of your life and realizing that this is what you have been missing out on your entire life. Imagine all of these beautiful desires and the amount of joy they will bring into your life. Now imagine that the moment you get them . . . you fumble them because you do not know how to properly maintain them. It doesn't sound much like joy anymore, huh?

All of these things sound amazing, but how could you really enjoy them if you have never learned to maintain them. Building success and having success in every area of your life does not happen overnight. It *requires* patience, dedication, commitment, and a lot of lessons that have to be learned.

Over the past 10 years in my career, I have learned some really tough lessons. I have made hundreds of thousands of dollars but needed to learn how to manage and save it properly. I have had fancy cars and beautiful apartments, but I had to truthfully learn to pay bills on time. I have been in relationships and thought I had met the love of my life, but I didn't know that I needed to truly heal my inner child who was hurting and needing healing. It was when I chose to do THE WORK that I got better results in my life. Everything great in life, I have had to put in real work and focus to actually maintain it. The best thing about God is that He is so gracious to walk with us side by side in our journey, leading us along the way.

Requirements are necessary to guide you toward your wildest dreams. Everything you want requires something in exchange for having and being able to maintain it. If you are looking to become an entrepreneur or build a successful business, you are required to show up every day. You are required to promote your business even when you have no customers. You are required to learn something new every day, either online or in a book. You are required to become a leader and invest in your craft. You are also required to build your customer service skills. These are non-negotiable things. You must learn these in exchange for a successful business with a ton of customers and people who trust you to provide them with quality service.

If you are looking to make a huge purchase, like a house or a car, you are required to save your money and focus on your credit. You simply need both. You must sacrifice something. If that means no shopping, no clubbing, or no fancy vacations for a while, that is the sacrifice you have to make short term to have what you truly want long term. In the process, it could seem challenging to make better decisions, but you have to see the bigger picture. You understand that you have to put in 10x the work to get 10x the results.

If you are a service provider looking to become the best at ANYTHING in your city, you must consistently push yourself to prove that you are the best. In order to make a name for yourself, you are required to make sure everyone in your city knows that you are the best at what you do and they should do business with you. You are required to pass out flyers, promote your business, and offer clients an experience of a lifetime. Before you know it, your entire city knows you, not because you are good at what you do but because you are consistent and your confidence speaks for you!

I named this Chapter: Luke 12:48 because I want you to keep this scripture in the forefront of your mind every time you start to question why it is so hard for you to reach your goals or achieve your heart's deepest desires. You can have anything and do anything in this world if you put your mind and your focus 100% on it. You are required to DO MORE, SHOW UP MORE, and understand that God needs you to show up as your BEST self when walking in the will He has for your life. You can do it.

CHAPTER

THE MILLION DOLLAR DREAM

I said it before, and I will say it again, I would loveeeeee to tell you that my journey has been so easy, and no challenges have caused me to lose faith and simply give up. It has not. I can not count the amounts of times I wanted to throw in the towel and call it quits. I've lost hope, struggled with confidence, and lost myself along the journey, but I have also gained strength, built confidence, and found myself along the journey. Success is a two-way street. You win some, you lose some.

The *Million Dollar Dream* simply starts with a Million Dollar Idea. Trust me, I understand that this is easier said than done, but using your imagination and creativity can take you so far. Being original and setting your intentions on being a problem solver is the easiest way to come up with a million-dollar idea or strategy. What is a problem that you see in your market? How can you solve it? What is a service you wish others provided that you can now offer?

Choosing to become a *"Dream Chaser"* was the best thing I could have ever done for myself! Think about when you were a child. Do you remember the first thing you honestly dreamed about becoming? A Famous Singer/Actor? Doctor? Nurse? Entrepreneur? Who or what created that dream for you? Was there anything or anyone that influenced or inspired that dream? Now fast forward to your now adulthood. Whatever happened to that dream? Did you chase it, or did you abandon it? What most need to understand is that having the dream is the easy part; chasing it can be difficult as it requires a LOT of hard work.

I've always dreamed of being an entrepreneur. I've always wanted my own money and my own business. Growing up, my mother was a Hairstylist/Entrepreneur, and my father was a Motivational Speaker/Author/Entrepreneur. I watched my parents chase their dreams and make things happen for themselves and their families. I watched them sacrifice time with loved ones to go after things that would benefit them in the long run. Everyone's marathon is different, and although I judge no one's hustle, I was proud that I grew up having a real dream and watching the people I love chase theirs.

Make a list of dreams that you are making a choice TODAY to chase endlessly. These can be dreams for your family, children, business, relationship, or anything you can think of.

Every day of my life, my mind is constantly racing, trying to come up with new ideas and new strategies to better myself and my business. I always spend most of my time both *innovating* and *creating*. This puts me so far ahead of the game and others in my industry because I'm spending time that others are not, building my brand. Not only is this important for you as a business owner, but it also sets the tone for the consumer you wish to attract. Your creative flow and your consistency are what will drive customers to your business to support YOU out of all of the others in your same exact industry.

At the start of my Million Dollar Journey, I knew and made a commitment to the fact that I would have to do all of the things that Millionaires do. Plain and Simple. Things that you think are common sense are only so common once you realize that you are the only person in your friend group doing it. This list of "requirements" contains things like reading books, watching informative podcasts, investing your money, actually budgeting and spending less money on unnecessary things, creating healthy boundaries in every aspect of your life, sacrificing some of your younger years so that you can live in abundance as you grow older, the list goes on. These habits are so important because they build the character needed to MAINTAIN SUCCESS.

Two books have helped me along my journey, and it is only fitting that I share them with you. "The Millionaire Booklet" and "The 10x Rule", both by Grant Cardone, have been my saving grace. These MUST HAVES created such a beast in me that I never knew existed. Grant Cardone and his wife, Elena Cardone, have been two of my inspirations along this journey because they literally give the game away while still being honest about the real struggle it takes to get here. There is no sugarcoating with them. The struggle is what made them tough, the sacrifice is what made them rich, and the wisdom is what made them WEALTHY. So yes, I am beyond inspired.

The first book I read by Grant was " The Millionaire Booklet." I read this book in less than 1 hour. It was THAT GOOD! On the last page of his book, he says, "And when you become a millionaire, make me the first person you contact!" These words gave me the exact push I needed to reach my goal of a Million Dollars in sales in 2023. Why? At that moment, he made me *believe* that it was possible. Believing is literally the first step to truly achieving the goal you have in mind. If you don't believe you can do it, you should put this book down right now. You are not ready.

Do you believe you have what it takes? Do you believe that you are a WINNER? Do you speak positivity into yourself? What thoughts and beliefs are currently limiting you?

Take a moment to write down a few of your beliefs, both positive and negative, when it comes to who you are and who you can become. Be as detailed as possible, and again, be HONEST. We are working toward something here, and

this may seem challenging, but I want to help you create a strong belief system, for this will serve as the foundation for who you can become.

Limiting beliefs are the only thing that can prevent us from pursuing our goals and living in our wildest dreams. These beliefs create false narratives about who we are and who we have the choice to become. The reason that I wanted you to write down both the great and not-so-great beliefs is that when you find yourself thinking negative thoughts or limiting yourself, these positive affirmations will help to get you back on track. I know that the mind can be a very tricky vessel, but we have the choice every day to turn every negative into a positive. Think positively on this journey, and the universe will align to give you everything possible under the sun simply because you believe that you are just deserving.

CHAPTER

Million Dollar Mindset: Overcoming Challenges

You wouldn't believe how much of your success is determined by the mindset you have. You can have all of the money, all of the resources, and all of the fame, but the mindset is what will sustain them all. Creating a mind that works FOR you instead of against you is one of the most challenging processes within this journey. Have you ever heard the saying, "Me vs. Me" or "My only enemy is the IN in me"? Get it?

Sometimes, our mind plays tricks on us, causing us to go back on everything we know to be true. The key to mastering your mind is going to be complex, but it could be so simple; *change your thoughts*. "Only positive thoughts and unconditional love exist here." Remind your mind of that every day. When you find yourself doubting your potential or questioning if you're moving in the right direction, do your best to take a moment, breathe, and know that every single thing that you want WANTS YOU BACK. Once you decide to make a change in any area of your life, nothing, and I mean nothing, can stop you.

I said I was going to be vulnerable, right . . . well, here we go. The first 6-8 months of 2022 were a very rough, dark, and lonely time for me. I mean, life was kicking my butt! Joy, Peace, and Bliss felt like complete strangers that I once knew and loved, while depression was indeed my best friend for a moment. I can't quite tell you what exactly was wrong because literally EVERYTHING FELT WRONG. I found the courage to finally let go of an on-and-off relationship that no longer served me. I began to truly pour my pain into purpose with my hair company. In the midst of still discovering who I was and who I wanted to become, I was a service provider, and my clients still expected me to show up as the person they grew to love on social media. This was extremely challenging.

I am a whole Sagittarius, ok. Freedom, Outdoors, Traveling, and Socializing are in my DNA. Let me paint the picture of the Evan-Nicole I once knew. I usually have an obsession with loving on myself. Prior to my space of uncertainty, I was rarely ever sad. I would cry about 3-4 times a year, and I can also, to a bittersweet fault, become so detached from heavy feelings or intense emotions that I tend to permanently block out everything negative or draining in my life. I am super fun to be around, and at my best, I am a burst of energy and always the life of the party. To see me down is to not see me because there is no way I'm coming out to hang with an attitude. Uh uh!

That was the Evan-Nicole I knew and loved, really the Evan-Nicole everyone loved . . . so can you see how this dark phase of my life was sooooooo painful and confusing because everything I knew and loved about myself began to change. I (in my mind) had no control over any of it. I started to stay in a lot more (I barely knew what "outside" was at this point). I began to take much-needed space from friends who no longer served this particular season of my life. I took a lot of losses in business, simply investing and seeing no return, and most importantly, I began to grieve my old life. Here I was, no longer 21, 22, or 23, enjoying my hot girl summer, but instead, I was turning 27 and preparing for my future. This took an emotional toll on me.

Thankfully, things were about to CHANGE drastically, and Lord knows, I had no idea what was waiting for me on the other side. Around mid-September, something in me just "woke up." It was like I had been in a deep sleep, dreaming the entire year because, for the first time in a long time, I was awake. I made a decision that I wanted to truly *live* and *be* in purpose. One night, I prayed to God, just asking for guidance and to be a waymaker in my journey. I needed him to lead my steps because I had no idea where I was going or where I was. Most importantly, I asked him to change my MIND and to release unto me a peace that allowed me to submit myself to His will for my life instead of my own. This prayer sounded a lot like this:

Dear God,

I need you. I am at a standstill, and I do not know which way to go. I am asking for You to intercede in my life by being a decision-maker and a way-maker. Grant me peace in the midst of my chaos and clarity in the midst of my confusion. I am tired, but I feel safe knowing my soul finds rest in You. I am lost, but I know that you will make a way out of no way. I surrender to your will for my life. I choose Your way and not my own. I know that only You know what is best for me, and I will trust in Your word because You are a promise keeper. Keep me. Guide me. Have your way. Amen.

Create a mantra for your mind. What are some things you wish you could say to your future self? Is there a prayer you have been asking God for that you would like to dig deeper into? Write it below.

_____

_____

_____

_____

Having a sound mind is something I ask God for daily. A mind that is clear and concise. A mind that doesn't play tug-of-war with my heart. A mind that doesn't harbor fear and abandon peace. I want a mind that is understanding of my journey but understands that submission to God's will is more important. A mindset like this has no choice but to walk in the divinity of PURPOSE. I choose peace every day, even on the days it feels like a foreign concept. I search for clarity in everything now. Literally everything. My relationships, my friendships, my workspace, even my decisions.

The Millionaire Mind, to me, is the mind that simply BEATS THE ODDS! It challenges every negative thought with a positive one! It believes in something and knows that as long as you continue to pursue, in confidence, the desires of your heart, it will manifest. The Millionaire Mind is a daredevil, always empowering itself to dream bigger and do more! This mind is the mind that will get you out of a 5-year funk and push you out of your comfort zone into a space of unconditional love and blessings.

The best part about this "mindset" is that you are the creator of it. Everything that you think, from this moment forward, can create the reality you experience. Choose peace today. Choose purpose today. Choose to live the life you deserve. I say deserve because although life doesn't come with a manual when walking in the plan God has for you finally goes right, you now have what I call "bragging rights." I brag about the favor God has over my life. Why? Because from birth, it was already written, but by will, all I ever had to do was *make it a choice*.

As you overcome the daily obstacles in your life, try to find at least one positive in every negative situation. Instead of always finding something that went wrong, think of something that went right. Instead of dwelling on the bad, try to find comfort in the good. Choose your battles wisely. Think of every battle you choose to face as a block to a blessing you have been asking God for (Trust me, this will make you rethink your choices). Learning to have this mindset in even just one area of life will pour into every area of your life, and you won't even notice it. You will walk away from every situation with no fight but somehow still undefeated because you have won the most important battle you will ever encounter in your mind.

To the woman or gentleman reading this, I pray that you gain control over your mind. I pray for less sleepless nights and more productive mornings. I know that on this journey to success, your mind can be one of the biggest battles you face. I want you to know that I understand and that you are not alone. We are all on this journey together, and often, you just need the reminder:

> *You are in control. You are worth it. You are capable. You are deserving. You are the MASTER of your Million Dollar Mind.*

Side Note:

When you get a second, please go to YouTube and listen to the Sermon titled "Push Through" by Sarah Jakes Roberts. This is a message that is on my heart to share with you right here, right now. She speaks about how the enemy will play tricks with your mind right at the peak of your breakthrough. He is fully aware of your traumas, your triggers, and even the calling God has over your life. He is clever in his attempts to play tricks on your mind because he knows it will delay your blessing that is waiting for you on the other side.

Today is July 27, 2023, and it is currently 5:03am. Your girl is exhausted, but my spirit is so refreshed. Please remember that I am just like you, and I've been where you are, hungry for more. As I continue on this journey of personal development, I am determined to master my mind while rebuking the enemy in the process. I understand the challenges that come with being called by the Most High, and as I sit here in tears from crying my eyes out from the amazing message she just poured, I realize something so special: *sometimes all we need is a PUSH.* Sometimes, all we need is that whisper that says, "You got this! You can do it! Keep pressing forward!" This message gave me that push.

CHAPTER

THE MILLION DOLLAR JOURNEY

I was 15 years young when I got my first and last job at Foot Locker. I loved everything about having a job. I was independent, I loved making my own money, and I enjoyed my co-workers. I knew immediately that I wanted to be my own boss because I hated being told what to do, and I was always late to work (IF I can be honest here). I worked as a cashier and learned so much about money and inventory, not realizing that one day I would own a warehouse for a Million Dollar Hair Company, still working with money and inventory.

I began my journey as an entrepreneur at the age of 17 years old. A new high school graduate on her way to college, I was determined to make some money. I continued to work at Foot Locker my last summer before I attended Hampton University for my freshman year. I saved all of my money and began to invest in all of the best flat irons and hot tools. I knew I wanted to do hair and immediately became the talked-about hairstylist on campus. Word of mouth and passing out business cards were the thing back then. There was no promoting yourself on Instagram and going "viral." I was straight up trapping out of the dorm room and loved every second of it!

Shortly after my freshman year, I returned home wanting to pursue the journey into entrepreneurship. I went back to my part-time job at Foot Locker to save up just enough money to start my quest to be a hairstylist. I immediately began to invest in business cards, products, hot tools, and anything you can think of that I would need to further this dream. I got my start by visiting different beauty supply stores, placing my business cards at the front desk, walking up to random women, giving them business cards, and even asking friends and family if I could do their hair for free in exchange for content and promo (although this worked back in 2013, I do not recommend this now). I had grown so accustomed to my clientele back at Hampton that I had to come home and basically start from scratch. I was actually putting in work if you ask me. Between using Foot Locker as a stepping stool and intense motivation to better myself, my clientele began to grow here in Atlanta, and as soon as I branded myself as The Hair Guru, the journey began.

Prior to gaining any sort of clientele, I actually needed a concrete plan. I knew what I wanted, but I was still determining how I would get there. Growing up, my mother owned a salon, Genesis Hair Art, which was almost like a big sister to me. I was what they would consider a "salon kid"; you know, the kids that are always in the salon with their mom? Yes, that was me! I watched her as an entrepreneur and knew one day I would be just like her! I would watch her slay her clients while selling products and also be a boss, writing checks to her commission-based stylists! This woman was a superhero in my eyes, and everyone loved her!

My mom would always keep all of her products on display in her salon and would always preach to me that retail is just as important as being a service provider. At the age of 19, something just told me to start selling e-commerce! I didn't have any idea what I wanted to sell, but I knew that people trusted my judgment as an influencer and would for sure buy anything hair-related that I would offer!

I wanted to find a product that I would use daily to make it easier to sell. I thought, "Hmm, HOT TOOLS! I would buy them at the wholesale price of $60–$90, then sell them at the retail price of "$129–$169"! I was profiting about $70-$80 each iron! This was good money back then! All I had to do was sell 6 irons to make around $600 and 12 irons to make over $1000! This was huge! I would use the few clients I did have to promote the actual product on social media, and for a while, I would just take orders via social media. I began to do a lot of research online and created my first website ON MY OWN. I used Vistaprint to create my business cards, flyers and began to pass them out everywhere! Malls, Beauty Supply Stores,

Nightclub bathrooms, anywhere I would go, a card would get left behind!

This lasted about 3-4 months, and then, one day, I saw a promotion for the Shaderoom for a $600 page post. Now, at the time, they only had 2.4 million followers, and the algorithm was much better, showing your post as soon as you post, so I knew it would be a good investment! About a week went by, and I scheduled my post for the following Friday. That Friday came, and while in Ikea with my dad shopping for furniture (because I had just moved out from my mom's place), I noticed my PayPal account blowing up! It was sale after sale after sale!!! I was 19 years old at the time, and in 1 day, I made $19,000, and in 1 week, I made $30,000, SELLING ONLY FLAT IRONS. This was iconic at my age! I made my very first 6 figures that year, and I knew I would be addicted to retailing products.

As my clientele and customers began to grow, so did the expansion of my mind! As I mentioned before, *to whom much is given, much is required.* My mind began to expand as an entrepreneur due to an entirely different experience. No more clocking in, no more limiting myself, and no more building a business for someone else; this time, I'm doing it for me! Now let me be transparent again, this process took work. Challenging my mind and everything I knew seemed so foreign to me. I made a lot of mistakes. As a hairstylist, I was late to appointments frequently due to no longer having that set schedule I once knew. I also didn't have my skills 100% perfect, so I made a lot of mistakes and tried my best to resolve them. I didn't expect the fast growth of my business, so I didn't have the full inventory to fulfill the orders! Although I had the funds, I needed to catch up on inventory for at least a month after that Shaderoom post! This was tough, but I was a work in progress FOR REAL.

Practice makes what? Perfect, you say? WRONG. Practice makes improvement, and you keep practicing until you improve and do it all over again. As the years progressed, things got better. Sales began to be consistent just as orders started to ship out on time. I began to wake up earlier, and as I perfected some of my techniques, I gained more and more clientele. The best teacher in life will be the lessons YOU learn, not the ones taught to you. Take every L as a lesson to better yourself and improve your current work ethic! Sure, you are going to fall short, and things may not go as planned, but these are the circumstances that build character and help to create longevity for the business you have.

I will be honest and say that it took me a while to truly enjoy "the journey." The reason I didn't truly enjoy the journey was because I didn't *understand* it. As you are growing in any area of your life, you are doing two things: stretching yourself into a new identity/dimension and building up the endurance to be able to compete with yourself at your next level! These two, together, are what most would consider too hard or too much. This is why only some people you meet will have a success story to tell. They may have given up, or they simply couldn't sustain the mental, emotional, and physical stretching this journey required.

By 23, I wrote my very first journal, The Guru Game Plan. This journal was a self-help/manifestation journal that gave readers an in-depth look at how I manifested the life I always wanted. It was my first ever published book, so yes, I was nervous, but I was so excited that I sold over 250 copies in less than 6 months! Another goal was checked off of the list! I had a huge book signing, and everyone, including my followers and supporters, showed up! This was such a massive milestone for me because it led me straight to the writing of this book.

Around 25/26, I wanted to push myself even further! I've always been into extensions but never had a consistent vendor or even knew where to start. I did a lot of research online and looked everywhere I could for the perfect vendor for my company. At the time, I was only familiar with Brazilian hair, so I narrowed down my search a bit. I invested a lot and lost a lot because there are far more bad vendors than there are good ones! Finding QUALITY in anything is like looking for the pot of gold at the end of the rainbow, but I was blessed by a friend of mine with a perfect vendor to get my start, and whew, this gave me a bit more faith to keep going.

I gave birth to Glam Affair Hair Co. on May 27, 2021, and I immediately began branding her. Website, Social Media Accounts, Hang Tags, Thank You Cards, Custom Packaging, anything branding-related, I was on it! I really believed that I could have a Million Dollar Hair Company FROM DAY 1! I knew that it was a far-fetched dream, but I also knew that it was possible. A girl like me, from the suburbs of Clayton County, just out here chasing her dream, but I knew I could do it! The little girl in me just had to!

On the first day of dropping my website, I anticipated a HUGE AUDIENCE! The website was beautiful, I launched a sale, the inventory was in and I was overly excited for this day. On Launch Day, I didn't sell 1 bundle of hair extensions. I don't think I sold anything that entire weekend. Would you believe it? All of the long months, the rush into getting inventory in by a specific date, the pushing back of deadlines only to NOT sell one bundle. This was a hugeeeee loss in my eyes. I felt defeated and overwhelmed. How am I pushing this product, pushing this launch, and no one showing up? This taught me what it meant to SHOW UP even when no one is buying! Yes, you do rely on your consumer for the sale, but you also rely on yourself to show up no matter what!

At this moment, I had to go back to the drawing board. Here I am, thinking I was fully prepared with everything I needed to start this business and be successful, but what I needed was a concrete plan, a marketing plan. Although I had experience in branding and marketing, I needed a marketing strategy for this business. I always knew how to sell, but I never knew how to truly MARKET. I realized almost immediately that I would have to dig deeper into owning a business and successfully launching it! Although every launch doesn't have to be big, it does have to be *planned.*

As I began creating a plan, a lightbulb went off, and I realized the most significant advantage of having this hair company: I am a hairstylist. Some of the biggest and most known hairstylists in the game don't own hair companies, and the majority of the hairstylists who are still working their way up don't either. This set me apart. I began to start promoting the hair using my clients. I would offer them a discounted service for purchasing my hair, and I would record content to post as an advertisement. After providing that discounted service, almost all of my clients began to purchase from me, and this helped a ton with my online sales for the people in other states who couldn't get the salon experience with me but still wanted to experience this hair!

A year went by, and I became really proud of my small wins. Each month, my company was growing in sales!

In February 2022, we only made $7000.
In July 2022, we made $27,000.

In November 2022, I began to invest in my business by running ads through Facebook and Instagram. This gave my business the extra push to be available to a broader spectrum of customers. We did $64,000 in sales that month, and by January of 2023, we were able to add another almost $20,000 to that, giving us a total of $86,000! By February, we hit our very first $100k month in sales! I couldn't believe it! The only month with 28 days was the exact same month God decided to show me that He would lead the way! By March, we were looking at $171,000 in sales! I was freaking out and losing my mind at the same time!

I wasn't freaking out because this was coincidental. I was freaking out because I finally started to see my hard work pay off! Everyone knew about Glam Affair Hair Co., and if they didn't, they would soon find out! I've had customers tell me that my ads bullied them into buying my hair! Although this was a funny comment, it made me feel good because that is what you want for your business! People should almost feel obligated to shop with you simply because it's in their faces! Running Ads skyrocketed my business, and here we are, 8 months into the year, almost at $1,000,000 in sales.

You know, they say that the first million is always the hardest. After that, it will never take that long again. Reaching this goal has been so personal to me because it technically didn't take 8 months; it took 10 years. 10 years of personal development, building, losing, winning, failing, succeeding, all of it played a part . . . for 10 years straight. I always wondered when God would do it for me, but it wasn't until I began to SHOW UP that God decided to SHOW OUT!

Becoming a hairstylist/entrepreneur changed my life in every way possible! It gave me real hope, a real challenge! I challenge myself in every way possible! I always try to double what I made last week the following week, and I always try to sell twice as many products today as I sold yesterday. On this journey, I began to set goals and really challenged myself to check them off of my to-do list! Having a 9 to 5 helped me to understand entrepreneurship more because although they are entirely different, I got to experience what it was like to both work for a million-dollar company and now own one. Wild, right?

CHAPTER

BUILDING THE MILLION DOLLAR TEAM

I have to always give credit where it is due, and I can never help but show love and gratitude to my team for helping me make all of my wildest dreams come true. My biggest thing when writing this book was to be sure I didn't gatekeep. I want you to know every step that is essential to your growth while building your business to a 7 figure business. Building a solid team is critical to any business owner who wants to achieve their goals. A team of talented and motivated individuals can help you to take your business to the next level.

When building your team, it is essential to consider the following factors:

- **The skills and experience that you need:** What skills and experience do you need in your team members?

Do you need people with technical skills, marketing skills, or sales skills? Having a clear vision of what exactly you need from your team will help you to choose the right people for the job.

- **The personality types of your team members:** It is crucial to have a variety of personality types on your team. This will help to create a more balanced and productive team environment. I am big on giving everyone on my team their own job. This allows each person to showcase their strengths, which will eventually help the business.

- **The values of your team members:** Your team members should share your values and goals. Creating a cohesive and motivated team should be your goal. Everyone needs to understand your vision to work at a high level of efficiency.

- **The communication skills of your team members:** Communication is essential for any team. The team you build must be able to communicate effectively with each other and with you. This helps to create an environment that has no choice but to thrive because everyone is comfortable enough to express ideas or concerns that could potentially help the business grow.

- **The motivation of your team members:** Your team members should be motivated to achieve your goals. This means that they should be passionate about your business and believe in your vision simply because they believe in you. Expanding your business can be challenging at the start, but as you build your team, remember you are looking for team players rather than business partners.

Now, here I am, being honest again . . . if I can live in truth for a moment, I didn't begin to build a team until I could *afford* one. For over a year and a half, I was on my own team. I played every role in my business: owner, branding manager, social media marketing, packager, order shipper, customer service representative, and every role you can think of, I played the part. This was such an important part of my journey because if I had never experienced each role, I wouldn't know how to hire and fire accordingly to now replace myself with someone who can do the job for me. This will now cost me money but save me time that I could be spending doing something else.

Building both a reliable and trustworthy team is so important. I first hired my best friend, Prescillia, as my assistant. This was an easy decision because I knew and trusted her for over the past 15 years of my life. This is someone who knows me like no other and has always been my right hand. I pointed out her strengths to determine where she would fit as a part of my business. She has been in both the corporate world and the service industry for quite a while, so I knew that she would do well in customer service. This was a huge relief for me, given I'm also a hairstylist, so I often experienced delays when responding to emails, texts, or phone calls.

When I say this girl held it down, she did her thing! I couldn't have asked for anyone better, honestly. At the time, I was still packing orders from home, and often, prior to working for me, she would watch and help if needed, so technically, she already knew what to do. Being a quick learner, I was able to guide her and correct mistakes when made, which also helped so that we wouldn't make the same mistakes twice. THIS IS REALLY IMPORTANT when choosing your team players to help you win!

I later hired a family friend who had previously worked with my mother for years. She has known me my entire life, so to have this full-circle moment really woke up the inner child in me. I knew that she would be able to pick up where I lacked. She had experience in customer service and also learned a lot about warehousing, something I had no clue about. The moment she stepped in, she treated my business as she would her own. Anything she didn't know, she researched, and this was a huge deal for me. I am big on educating myself, and if I don't know it, I know someone who does: GOOGLE. Hiring her has changed so much of my business because I learned things at a faster pace, having multiple eyes and ears to help me carry the vision.

Having effective communication skills can also go a long way as the CEO and when choosing your employees. When mistakes are being made or customers are a bit feisty about their orders, you must be able to both correct and coach your team on how to handle these problems so that when they arise, your staff is prepared. You are so much better and stronger as a team than by yourself. If you can package 25 orders by yourself, you can package 250 orders with the help of your team. Creating this system can be tricky without proper guidance, but if you trust God and yourself, you will make significant decisions and learn so much along the way.

Growing my team was not the easiest, but being able to trust that they would make things happen without me micromanaging them was a challenge. I was so used to doing it all myself for the past 10 years, so I knew what I liked and how I liked it. It was my way or no way. I always knew I wanted a complete team that could help run my business, but I needed the territory to do so. Running a business out of a 2 bedroom apartment was not easy, but for 2 years, it worked, and I told myself that once I outgrew the space, I would invest in a warehouse and trust that God would lead me along the way. Always be content with exactly where you are. You don't have to have a massive warehouse or the $100k sales/month to run a successful business. It starts with the backend. It begins with the foundation of the business, and as the foundation gets stronger, one day, you'll look up, and the entire business will be built and stable.

What are some of your strengths? What are some of your weaknesses? If you were to build your Million Dollar Team, what would be some of the qualities and values you look for in them? How could they balance out your weaknesses?

CHAPTER

Million Dollar Marketing Guru

Marketing as a business owner is and should be your best friend. Marketing is the activity or business of promoting and selling products or services, including market research and advertising. Now again, here I am, being honest. Marketing is going to take a lot of work at the start, but it is something that you can build a relationship with. Marketing can benefit your business in so many ways because it allows you to reach an audience that you wouldn't get otherwise.

Marketing can include strategies such as Ads, Email and SMS Text Marketing, Billboards, and even Social Media for Blogs and Influencer Marketing. Each strategy has its benefits, and depending on the business you have, one strategy may serve you better than another. The best way to decide which strategy is best for you is to determine: WHO IS YOUR AUDIENCE? This is beyond significant because no matter what strategy you choose to use for your business, you have to decide which one would best capture your desired audience.

My top marketing strategy right now that scaled my business to over $100k a month is Facebook, Instagram, and TikTok ads. Because I had no idea how to do this, I did my research to find the best marketing company to run ads, secure sales, and help my business reach bigger audiences. Running ads as an e-commerce business is very helpful because it puts your business in the faces of people who may shop online. When creating an online store, you want to be able to sell to customers in other states. Your potential customers may be in different states or may prefer an online experience. Hence, this strategy helps to better reach them.

Email and text marketing are two of my favorite strategies for my hair company. It is cost-effective and entirely permission-based. Unlike running Ads, this strategy offers a more personal solution to interacting with your *desired* audience. When a customer opts in to receive your SMS text messages and emails, they are already interested in the product you have to offer. You are now able to personalize a campaign that will be sent directly to their phone. This opens the door for quicker and more strategized sales. Consumers begin to feel like more of a VIP customer when they discover that they're getting first dibs on all of the upcoming sales and promotions your company is offering. This is my favorite because it is really effective when planning sales and campaigns by immediately notifying the customer in case they don't see what you or your brand may post online.

Billboards are also an amazing marketing strategy that can help potential customers see your business while simply driving home or on the way to work, the spa, the gym, or any areas of high traffic. Billboard marketing can cost anywhere from $2,000 to $20,000 per month, based on location. The impressions can also vary based on where the billboard is located. My very first billboard was a gift to me in February 2023. It was located on Piedmont Ave., which is a very high-traffic area here in Atlanta. The impressions were between 200,000 to 250,000 views a week. I was stoked! Not only did this bring brand awareness, but I was also able to promote a sale using the code BILLBOARD and ask customers to find the billboard for an additional percentage off. (of course, I offered them hints!)

The last and final marketing strategy that will forever be my go-to would have to be social media! Social media has changed everything about the way I market because, unlike all of the other strategies, customers are looking for consistency on social media. As a consumer, they want to be able to come to your page and see exactly what you have to offer. Some customers may even watch your brand for months, even years, up until they decide to support it. This is a good thing. In fact, it's an advantage. Consistently posting your content and filming your journey allows your customers to connect with you long-term in an authentic way. If you are a hairstylist, lash technician, makeup artist, or even a photographer, people want to see your work! They want to see you posting your clients' experiences as well as building up that momentum in your business! They want to know the good and the bad, and luckily, if you're anything like me, the good will outweigh the bad every time.

No matter what strategy you decide to use for your business, you must understand that no matter if you are a small business, just starting up, or a 6–7-figure business, you must find your target audience and gravitate to them. Go where it flows. You can not grab everyone's attention simply because everyone may want something else. Knowing who your audience is and what they are looking for speeds up the process of making careless mistakes while marketing. If you take your time and put in the work to actually cultivate your strategies, you will see that it gets easier and more effective as you learn what does and does not work.

Who is your target audience? What are some things that only you could offer to them that no other company can? Which strategy would best benefit your business?

I understand what you may be thinking, "ok, she's talking about this campaign thing, but what is that, and where do I start?" This was me about a year ago. I had yet to learn what it would take to run a successful business campaign. If you have never heard of it before, I'm telling you now that Google will be your best friend! Anything I ever need help with, I research. I am big on education and always looking to learn something new! Choose to teach yourself things that you need to become more familiar with. You can do this by searching on Google, reading books, or listening to audible and even podcasts. There is so much information out there for you. All you have to do is look for it.

One of my favorite marketing campaigns that I, along with my brand manager, created was our Black Friday/Cyber Monday Campaign, "The Hustle Affair." This campaign was created with one thing in mind: we wanted our customers to SPEND their money while making sure that they felt like they were getting an excellent deal! We didn't want to do a 1 or 2-day sale because everyone expects that with Black Friday/Cyber Monday. We extended it for the entire weekend so that no one felt like they missed the sale if they were tired or too busy from shopping in stores. We created content based off of what we were pushing to our customers. This can be anything from a photoshoot to a 30-second video clip promoting your products.

We are currently in a generation where, in order to put yourself or your business out there, you must use social media as a source. Now, this may only be for some, but as times change, so do trends. As the years have progressed, so has every social media platform. From Myspace to Facebook, Instagram, TikTok, and Twitter, this social media world is evolving. I understand that creating content is not easy, and neither is *being* a content creator. A lot of the things that I am suggesting to you to take your business to the next level will require some form of practice. We're going to dive a bit deeper into this.

I first began to create content at 19 years old when I began selling flat irons! I would ask someone to record while I pressed the hair out to show off how well the iron worked on coarse hair. This would help me with my sales because I was actually showcasing my product. I was taking a problem that most women with coarse hair would have, being not able to get their hair straight from root to end in one pass, and showing them that with my product, it was possible! This was an everyday thing that I would do, and my sales were through the roof! This taught me early on how important it was to make sure that you are pushing your product in a way that puts it in your consumer's face!

Now, I move in precisely the same way with my current business. Being a hairstylist for the past 10 years, I knew that one day I wouldn't want this to be my forever career. I want to branch off more into entrepreneurship and create a business that will sustain me for the rest of my life. I started Glam Affair Hair Co. with that goal in mind. The biggest advantage I had when launching this business was that I was also a hairstylist. Most people who own hair companies don't necessarily "do hair," so this was an advantage in my eyes because who better to promote hair than a HAIRSTYLIST?

I wanted to push the hair company as much as I could as long as I was still doing hair. I began to offer my clients a discounted price on their service for purchasing my hair at retail price. This worked well for me because, as a stylist, I had no issue taking a bit of a loss on a service I could always increase to temporarily build a business that would one day work for me. This strategy was truly a win-win situation because I still got paid for the service while also being able to get clients in my hair, build up customer satisfaction, and create dope content.

Creating a strategy that works for you is much more than discounting yourself or running a huge sale; it's figuring out the pros and cons of that strategy and seeing how it would, in the end, benefit the long-term goals you have in mind for the company. No matter which route you go, you have to make marketing your best friend! Marketing your business is just as important as branding your business. They go hand in hand. You brand to create familiarity with your business. At the same time, you market to push your potential consumers into making their first purchase.

Suppose you are currently looking to push a brand that you have already created. What strategies are you open to trying or developing that would greatly benefit the business?

_____
_____
_____
_____
_____
_____
_____

CHAPTER

THE POWER OF NETWORKING

Now, every other chapter has been my favorite, but this chapter actually means a lot to me. As I co-pilot you on this journey, I want you to know and truly understand that this journey is only for the WINNERS. Yes, winners take L's too, but while a loss to a loser is still a loss, a loss to a winner will always be considered a LESSON. As you grow in both your personal and business life, you will realize that people will fall off along the ride. The friends you once loved and cared for will no longer relate to you. The people you once dated will probably not even be your type anymore, and you will outgrow EVERYTHING AROUND YOU.

Building your network is a lot different from building your team. Your team will be the people who work for you with the same goal in mind for your business, while the network you create will be a stepping stone and a way to leverage who you are in your industry. There are so many benefits that come from networking, such as gaining access to new opportunities, learning from others, and building credibility. Have you ever heard the saying, "Ballers hang with ballers, Doctors hang with doctors, lawyers hang with lawyers"? Or what about, "Show me your 5 closest friends, and I'll show you where you'll be in 5 years"? This is all true.

Networking can help you find new potential clients or even business partners. It can also help you stay up-to-date on the latest trends and learn from other entrepreneurs. Your network should consist of people who can inspire and better you. Sometimes, it's not what you know. It's WHO you know. Creating relationships with people who are also successful in both their personal and business lives will help you to better yours by setting a tone for the things that you want and don't want.

My network became more important to me than just surface-level friendships and relationships. For years, I asked God to introduce me to people with the same business mindset as me and people who would push me to reach new heights. I wanted substantial friendships in my life that didn't just show up for me but they knew how to show up for themselves. They would be goal-oriented and understand that collaboration is always 10x better than competition. They would support me instead of criticize me when I had to make tough decisions, such as not going to the latest concert, not going to the club, or creating a budget to set myself up for financial success. This was such a pivotal moment for me because as soon as I asked, God began to send them my way.

As I started to let go of what I knew and change my vibration to match what I wanted, I began to attract like-minded individuals. Some of my closest friends right now are people I built a business relationship with first. These are people I can talk about everything with; money, business, life, love, and everything in between. Your network won't always become your best friends, but they will always be people you can lean on. The part that I love the most about this is that it will always be a two-way street. This is how you know that you're actually creating substantial connections. You will also be able to pour from your cup because you will always be full. You won't feel drained from being around a great network of people. You will be able to give and receive in this dynamic because everyone is on the same frequency.

> *"Networking is not about who you know, it's about who knows you."*
> —MARK CUBAN

Now, while I mention that networking is mainly about finding people who can better you and inspire you, it is also essential to be aware of how you can better and inspire someone else. You want to always be working towards becoming the best version of yourself because that is the only way you will maintain these relationships. You are your only competition. You are the only person who can hold you back. Therefore, building yourself up is so important when thinking of connecting with other people because you have to give people a real reason to want to connect with you. Of course, you won't attract everyone, but it makes it easier when you are aware of the type of people who will simply "get you."

There are a few things you should avoid when networking. For example, don't be too "salesy" or self-promotional. You never want to sell yourself to people. When networking, you can't be too selfish. Everything cannot always be about you. If you already know a bit about the person you want to network with, take a moment to see how you could best benefit them instead. If you are meeting someone for the first time at an event or a social gathering, try to connect. Find similar interests between the two of you; maybe you both do hair, or you're both into e-commerce; find a similarity and think of ways you could collaborate to better both of your businesses.

As a hairstylist, I love to invest in classes to educate myself on the newest techniques. I am so big on finding a hairstylist whose work I admire and reaching out to see if they offer either one-on-one or virtual classes. I'll shoot a DM, or if their booking link is open and available, I'll simply just book the class. I am open to traveling to meet them and paying for the classes or services. This is a good tactic I use when I want to connect with other talented women or men in my exact same industry because if they weren't familiar with me or my brand before, they are now.

Remember, your network is here to better you. A few places you could visit to build your network would be places where you think successful people are: the gym, industry events, sports games, etc. You can even reach out via social media to people you admire or would just like to connect with. Never be afraid or feel intimidated by reaching out first! You are the boss; therefore, you call the shots! Build your network around core values and make sure that they value the same things you do, whether it's in life, love, or business. Stay true to who you are and show up as your most authentic self, and you will meet some of the most amazing people in your life.

CHAPTER

Million Dollar Balance: Business vs. Personal

Although I am very outgoing and open about my business life, my successes, and my failures, I am more of a private person when it comes to my personal life. Behind every successful person are a lot of painful moments that have shaped and cultivated the person they are today. Speaking for myself, I had an amazing childhood and upbringing. I was blessed with amazing parents, a supportive family, and making friends and getting good grades wasn't much of a challenge for me. Being an only child was the most bittersweet challenge of them all. I faced a lot of my more challenging lessons once I was over 21.

Becoming an adult is a challenging transition for everyone. In the past 5–7 years of my life, I learned so much about myself and people in general. I've had a lot of personal experiences that have really hurt me, but looking back, they created a beast out of me. Pain became more of a *Motivational Guide* for me. From fake friendships to betrayals in relationships and even bad business partnerships or corrupt customers in my business, every situation that went bad became a motivation for me and allowed me to turn it into something good.

Have you ever heard the saying, "Never mix business with personal"? Well, I have. My mother instilled this in me the moment she began to notice I wanted to become an entrepreneur. I'm sure she also heard it before, but she was also saying it from her personal experience. This saying is true indeed, but it could have a few different meanings based on perspective. It could mean not mixing business relationships with personal pleasure, not taking personal feelings into your business dealings, or even keeping your personal life and your business life completely separate so that you can enjoy the fruits of your labor in both. Each perspective is solely based on where you are in your life, but they are all true.

Mixing business and personal pleasure can have a very negative outcome when owning a business because often, we need to pay more attention to the business aspect based on our personal experience. This can be in relationships or friendships, but both do apply. On your journey to 7 figures, you will quickly realize that business and personal won't mix. It is crucial to truly separate the two in order to make decisions that are in the best interest of your business successfully and strategically. Hiring and firing based off of personal feelings can be detrimental to your business because feelings aren't facts. Building your team around actual strategy and knowing what your business needs are the only ways success can happen.

When running a business, it can be easy to get caught up in the work field while neglecting your personal life. But it's important to make time for the things that are important to you, such as your family, friends, and hobbies. Building a 7 figure business isn't the most fun while your personal life is falling apart, and maintaining a happy personal life is challenging when business seems to be running slow, or customers are complaining. Having grace with yourself and learning to invest in both parts of your life is essential for creating a balance between your personal and business life.

Here are some things you can do to find a balance between your business and personal life:

- **Set boundaries.** Decide how much time you're willing to work and stick to it. This can look like putting your phone down or even on Do Not Disturb after 10pm. This can also look like creating a to-do list and knocking off as much as you can within a specific time frame and completing the rest another day.

- **Delegate tasks.** Don't try to do everything yourself. We talked a lot about building a team; use this to your advantage. Take some work off of you by putting some of the work off on them. This will make it easier for you to accomplish more in an area that may need your undivided attention.

- ▶ **Take breaks.** Get away from your work and relax regularly. Go to the spa or the gym, or better yet, have a drink at the bar across the street! There is so much more to life. Take breaks from work and do your best to actually enjoy them.

- ▶ **Spend time with loved ones.** Make time for the people who are important to you.

- ▶ **Do things you enjoy.** Make sure to make time for the things that make you happy.

As you and your business grow, you will begin to experience challenges that are meant to build you into the Boss and CEO you are meant to be. Who you become as a person is the most essential part of this journey. I can not stress that enough. Learning balance is so critical to your growth because it keeps you humble while still being hungry for more! Having a balance between your personal life and who you are in business is key to always maintaining a joyful work/life balance. I have experienced some of the best highs and even the most traumatic lows being a woman and a business owner. Still, I wouldn't trade any of it because they taught me BALANCE.

If you want to free up your time so that you can focus on the most critical aspects of your business, you also need to be willing to delegate tasks to others. Suppose you are an entrepreneur who has been used to doing everything yourself. In that case, this can be very difficult for you. Still, it's essential if you want to achieve your business goals without sacrificing your personal life. We spoke about building a team in Chapter 5 for this exact reason. Once you put other people in place to help you run your business, you avoid burnout while also making room for your personal life to flourish.

My biggest advice to you will always be to CHOOSE YOU. In any and every circumstance, especially in business, choose you. Choose your peace, choose your health, and choose all the things that make you happy. Never consume yourself so much with who you are as a business owner rather than who God called you to be. You are more than just a CEO; you are a daughter/son, a mother/father, and a friend.

Most importantly, you are human. We all go through this life with its trials and tribulations, but it is up to you to create balance through it all. You are capable, and it is possible.

What are the biggest challenges that you face in trying to balance your business and personal life?

What are some specific strategies that you can create to set boundaries between your work time and your personal time?

CHAPTER

Defining Your Success: The Art of Becoming

Between family pressures and even social media comparisons, so many people will tell you or make you think that you should be successful, but what does that truly mean? Success has a different meaning for every single person. For some, it may mean achieving financial prosperity. In contrast, for others, it may mean achieving personal fulfillment, making a difference in the world, or building strong relationships. The meaning of success is to each its own. Do not allow anyone to decide what that means or looks like for you!

There are so many benefits to defining your own success, such as increased motivation, personal development, increased clarity and clear direction. There are also a ton of dangers that come with comparing yourself to others and trying to achieve someone else's definition of success.

Allowing someone to create what success looks like for you will cause you to chase dreams that aren't even yours, and there is nothing worse than that. If success only looks like the perfect Instagram life, nice cars, a luxury high-rise, and a million dollars to you, I can tell you now that you are in for a rude awakening! Although all of those are nice, and we all want to experience a life of luxury, that should not be the GOAL.

For example, I have always loved nice and expensive things, but "things" have never been the goal. My goal has always been more about the lifestyle I wanted to create for my future children and my family. I have always wanted money to take care of my family and to be able to provide my future children a life that they won't have to heal from. I wouldn't want them to grow up saying, "My parents were struggling." Although that is a stigma in a lot of ethnic communities, I did not want that to be a stigma for me.

Having that mindset and understanding that the money WILL COME is what allowed the "things" to fully manifest. We all deserve nice things, 5-star vacations, and luxury experiences, but that should be different from your direct interpretation of what success is. Success is about defining what is important to you and then living your life in a way that allows you to achieve it. As you create and search for an understanding of what success means to you, you will begin to learn so many things about yourself. Becoming successful takes work! It's actually one of the hardest things to do. It requires hard work, sleepless nights, and a lot of risk-taking! According to research, 98% of people die without fulfilling their goals and dreams, leaving only 2% of people to truly become successful in life.

Some people feel successful after getting the dream family they've always hoped for! I love that for them! The reason why is that there are so many other perspectives of success outside of only financial gain. Finding your person, getting married and creating a family could bring someone all of the happiness money can't buy. This is important because it takes financial success out of the equation. Don't get me wrong, yes, it is highly recommended to be financially stable in order to provide a life for your family, but what life would it be if *money* was the only thing keeping the family together?

The best way to define your own success would be to set goals and create a vision for your future. This can look different for everyone, but I suggest that:

#1 Decide what it is precisely that you want. Be specific. What dreams are you trying to make a reality for you? What are some habits you would like to create in your life?

#2 Then, plan short-term, mid-term, and long-term goals. I personally like to plan by quarters. Every year, I plan the next 3 months of my life in hopes of doing things with both intention and purpose to lead me closer to my goal.

#3 Create deadlines for yourself. No one is going to hold you more accountable than you! You have to be your biggest cheerleader in this season! Create realistic deadlines for yourself and congratulate yourself when you make them, but also reprimand yourself when you do not. This could be congratulating yourself with a spa day or a staycation at a nice hotel in your city. It can also look like reprimanding yourself by sacrificing something you love until you reach the next deadline for that goal. For example, giving up eating out, shopping, drinking alcohol, going out to the bar/club/lounge, or even putting your phone on DO NOT DISTURB after 9pm/10pm to get rid of any distractions that may be hindering you.

Always be sure to acknowledge and celebrate your progress and achievements along the way. There is no better feeling than smashing your goals and keeping yourself motivated along the way! This is beyond important in order for you to feel great about yourself while also being inspired to keep going! I also encourage you to enjoy your journey to personal growth without just focusing on the destination. Trust me, with these steps, you will get there, but the most important part is who you become along the journey. You must become a person who is deserving of all of the amazing things that you want for your life.

Personal growth is the foundation of success and a lifelong endeavor. When you grow as a person, you expand your capabilities and open up new possibilities for yourself.

This is especially important when you're building a 7-figure business, as it requires you to step outside of your comfort zone and take on new challenges. The *Art of Becoming* is literally what all millionaires will tell you; it is the most important part of the journey to success. Your main goal should always be to be better, become a person of integrity, value, and substance. Who you become is far more important than the accolades and achievements you receive.

As you become who you are called to be, you will face many challenges while also learning from your experiences. Keep this from distracting you from reaching your goals! Every opportunity for you to learn from your mistakes is an opportunity that will be worth it in the long run! Do not run from any challenge, but instead, decide to face it head-on. There are NO EXCUSES in business. If there is a problem, find a solution. It is up to you to make your dreams come true, no one else. Become the person deserving and watch how God works in your favor.

List a few of your *short-term (3–6 months) goals* below. What are some steps that you can take today to put you one step closer to accomplishing these goals?

_____

_____

Chapter 9 | 72

List a few of your *mid-term (1–2 years) goals* below. What are some steps that you can take today to put you one step closer to accomplishing these goals?

List a few of your *long-term (3–5 years) goals* below. What are some steps that you can take today to put you one step closer to accomplishing these goals?

CHAPTER

God's Plan: The Million Dollar Celebration & Building a Legacy

August 17, 2023 11:04 PM

Journal Entry:

"Wow. Simply Wow.

There are no words to express what I'm feeling God.

WE DID IT JOE!

$1,000,462.74 in Sales as of 10:05pm.

God, THANK YOU for hearing me. Thank you for cheering me on. Thank you for guiding me. Thank you for protecting me. Thank you for gifting me a team, without them, none of this would be possible for me. You knew all along, huh? I guess I just had to go through a few things first to be sure you trusted me at this very moment. As the tears roll down my eyes, I can't think of anything but how grateful and blessed I am. I am so overwhelmed with emotions and I can't quite explain how I feel.

You did it for me, God. For little ole me, from the Southside of Atlanta.

If I can do it, I know I can inspire so many to do it. God lead me on this next journey, for I know now that my mission is bigger. I don't call myself GURU for no reason!!!! This is my WHY!

This first million will be the first of MANY. I have no doubts. I can't believe that tomorrow, when I wake up, I'll be the owner of a Million Dollar Hair Company. You outdid yourself with this one. BIG GOD, for a BIG GURU!

With love and gratitude, your favorite girl,

Guru"

For all of August, I manifested heavily as my hair company was about $30k away from our goal of a Million Dollars in sales. I was heavily journaling and also putting in the work. On August 17, 2023, my entire life changed. As I'm at my salon space, curling my very last client, I notice a sale from Shopify come in. I didn't immediately check it because my hands were pretty tied up, but once I finished my client and began to check her out, I was reminded of that sale. As soon as she left, I crossed my fingers while going back to the Shopify App to see if that sale was the sale that would cross my business over into a 7-figure status. I was so nervous because I didn't know if I would be disappointed or not.

The moment I pressed refresh and saw my sales hit over a million dollars, my eyes lit up, and I couldn't hold back the tears. They were immediate. As I walked back into my salon space, I asked my Amazon Alexa to play "If I Could Have Anything" by Housefires. As the song played, the spirit of God truly took over. The amount of gratitude and love I had in my heart was overwhelming. This was not about the number for me; it was about the faith I had carried the last 7 months of being a business owner.

Every trial. Every tribulation. Every tear. Every question. Every worry. Every self-doubting thought. Every sleepless night. Every sacrifice. Every single experience that made absolutely no sense to me at some point finally became crystal clear. Every risk. Every chargeback. Every difficult customer. Every day, I didn't have a team. Every moment of feeling defeated. None of it mattered anymore. It all felt worth it. The feeling was a feeling I prayed for months and months, time and time again. I could never forget it.

Remember that list you made in Chapter 1? The list of all of the things you are believing God for in the next season of your life? I want you to take a moment to simply imagine how you would *"feel"* the moment that dream became a reality? How will you feel driving that brand new car out of the dealership? What emotions come to your mind when you think about seeing your business finally hit $1,000,000 in sales? Honestly, think about it. What feelings or emotions come to mind when you visualize that God has done exactly what He said He would do?

Take a moment to list them below.

The reason I want you to identify these feelings is because one day, these exact feelings you've written down will be your reality. One day, you will look up, and you'll be living in the prayers of today. Visualizing is the first step. You have to SEE IT THROUGH. Please use my life and my story to motivate and further challenge you to keep reaching for the stars. Do not compare; everyone's journey will be different, but it will make sense to YOU and that is all that matters.

The most crucial part of success is the vision you have for yourself. In order to have the financial success you are looking for, you have to truly visualize and make peace with knowing that anything you want in this life wants you back. There are NO EXCEPTIONS. That is the rule. That is the law of attraction. The vision is what has always been so clear for me. I always knew that everything that I am currently experiencing in business at this exact moment would happen. I would daydream about the kind of car I wanted to drive. I would search Pinterest night and day to visualize how I wanted my warehouse to look. I also would listen to music that really put me "in my bag" just to speak greatness over my life. There was always this knowing of what God would one day do in my life.

So many of my years being "20-something" were honestly spent building the woman I am now. For the past 10 years, I have made sacrifices that have led me to this exact time, this very moment. I wanted to be as transparent as possible when writing this because I know that everything that glitters isn't gold. I want to set realistic expectations for you to truly succeed and avoid making the same mistakes I did. God's plan for you is so big you wouldn't possibly be able to believe it until you woke up one day living in it. Your only job is to believe that with your whole heart.

Building my business to 7 figures has been such a roller coaster of emotions because of all of the trials and tribulations that got me here. When you genuinely think about it, the reward is amazingly and exceedingly beyond your human expectations. It is almost as if there is this supernatural power that you can't see, working time after time to make your life better! Even when I think, "It can't get any better than this," it does. This is when you know you have reached true success in your life; things are working in your favor. This can be in any area of your life, but the feelings and emotions are real.

The reason I titled this Chapter "God's Plan" is because this is what it all boils down to. I can't be any more transparent with you in this chapter without you fully understanding what this means. God's plan is the ONLY plan that will work when believing Him for his grace and glory over your life. HIS PLAN over YOURS. The best part about His plan is that it comes with a lot less commotion and a lot more blessings. There is nothing that God can not and will not do for you. I pride myself on fully believing that He is a WAY MAKER and a PROMISE KEEPER. There has not been one thing in my journey that I've lacked after deciding to do things His way.

I can also be very open and honest with you and tell you that even in my space of unwavering gratitude, I have battled with my faith. I always say my faith outworks my hustle. Still, I also understand that it is challenging to always be faithful in times of uncertainty. Still, it is pivotal that you make a choice to believe in yourself and in God's capabilities. For many of my mothers' or soon-to-be mothers reading this, there is a legacy behind you depending on you to make the best decisions now for their future. It is your responsibility to build your empire along with your faith to be sure that their journey is built on a solid foundation.

I am personally not a mother, but I make every decision now with my future children in mind. The moment God decides to make motherhood a part of my journey, I am confident that I will have made decisions in my life that will set the standard of determination and perseverance in their life and affect who they become along their own journeys. "It will all make sense one day" is the motto. My success is for more than just me. It is for everything and everyone that will come after me. It is to make sure that my parents, grandparents, and great-grandparents are proud of the legacy they will one day leave behind.

Success is endless and no matter what people make it seem like on social media, everyone's journey will be different because everyone's starting point is different. My ancestors had different resources to accomplish the same goals as me. While the world continues to evolve, my children and grandchildren will have way more opportunities on their journeys to thrive while possibly doing less work. As I take inspiration from the people and situations around me, I begin to look at the glass as half full versus half empty. I am well aware of the idea that some people also have no idea *where* to start. The key to this is to simply just start. Start exactly where you are. Create goals and dreams for yourself exactly where you are. Make progress daily right where you are. Show up in any capacity and watch God show out for you.

Hitting a MILLION dollars in sales in 7 months for a company that is only 2 years old is a HUGE accomplishment. Although I am just now in a space to truly bask in the glory of it, I'm also reminded that this is only the beginning. This is only the beginning of my faith journey. This is only the beginning of what my 7/8-figure business will look like. This is only the beginning of the chapter of my life where I am proud. This is the beginning of the celebration, and the best part is that there is no end.

Every goal that you make for yourself and pursue endlessly to accomplish will only be another beginning chapter to the next part of your journey. Your success will be different from this book. It won't end in chapter 10. Instead, it will go on and on and on, and only you get to decide if and when you stop adding to each chapter. It is all up to you. Look at every accomplishment as not the end of the completion but a beginning and a start to only more greatness, more achievements, and a whole new ball game.

As you transition from a small-business owner to a 7-figure business owner, you'll encounter a unique set of challenges that demand a higher version of you and your entrepreneurship skills. Hitting this goal was a massive milestone for me in my personal life, but who the business forced me to become as a 27-year-old African American woman entrepreneur is what brought the most significant challenges. With no mentor, no handouts, and no "do or don't" list, every risk taken forced me to coach myself.

One of the primary challenges you'll face is scaling your operations to meet the demands of a rapidly expanding business. The complexities of running a large-scale enterprise will test your leadership skills, decision-making abilities, and capacity to manage a growing team. Some of the challenges I faced while dealing with the growth of my business were maintaining inventory, production and processing time, maintaining consistent growth, staying on top of marketing and promotion, hiring and firing, and customer satisfaction. On top of operating a fast-scaling business, I also had to maintain my clientele as a popular hairstylist in Atlanta, all while still trying to make time for my personal life.

As my business grew, so did my expenses. Managing cash flow effectively became crucial. I had to sacrifice unnecessary spending in order to develop a deep understanding of financial management skills. The challenges of budgeting, reinvesting, and organizing payroll all began to take a toll on me. No one seems to talk about the emotional toll of leading a high-growth business. The pressure to maintain momentum, meet ambitious targets, and satisfy a growing customer base can be overwhelming. I also had to develop robust coping mechanisms, cultivate a growth mindset, and surround myself with a supportive network to navigate the inevitable ups and downs.

I honestly am so excited that this is the start of a *new* journey for myself and my business. I'm reminded daily of the hunger I had when I first started and my goal is to have that same devotion and motivation for as long as I am on this earth. I have been living in prayers and manifestations since 2 years ago. This is no coincidence.

As I finish this book, I write in tears as I think about you, the reader, and pray that God shows you just how good it can get. God is blessing us every day. With every breath in our body and each day, we get the opportunity to make our next 24 hours better than the last. We are blessed. I pray that on this journey, you are reminded of how valuable you are and how much this world needs YOU. This world is yours. God is a God of ABUNDANCE. Everything here that God has equipped you with is for your good, and He will be your guide. You are the next millionaire in your family, and if you are the next AND the first, God is going to make this journey EPIC and mind-blowing for you. Face each challenge head-on and know that God has not given you the spirit of fear but of power, love, and a sound mind.

As you embark on your own Million-Dollar Affair, remember that the journey is just as important as the destination. Embrace the challenges, celebrate the victories, and never stop growing. Your personal growth is the foundation of your brand's success. Remember, the true wealth lies not in the numbers on a bank statement but in the richness of your experiences, the depth of your connections, and the indelible mark you leave on the world. Continue to learn, evolve, and inspire, and you will undoubtedly achieve greatness. Thank you so much for joining me on this journey of personal growth and entrepreneurial success. You have the tools and inspiration you need to create a life of fulfillment and abundance. Now go forth and make your million-dollar mark on the world!

With heartfelt wishes for your success,

Evan-Nicole "The Hair Guru" Williams

To the reader:

"I pray that you find true peace and acceptance in the space of uncertainty. I pray that in this current season of your life, God takes His time to mold you into who He has called you to be in your next season. I pray for your heart of gratitude, that you see all of the good for exactly what it is, and that you rest in knowing that the bad will work out for your good. I pray that God comforts you during every sleepless night and with every tear you shed. This journey will not be easy, but it will be rewarding. I pray that this book sticks with you through your journey and that you are reminded of His grace, His love, and His voice. He won't fail you."

—Amen.

Afterword

By Jonathan Williams (Dad)

As I pen the afterword to my daughter's remarkable book, "A Million Dollar Affair: A Guide to Personal Growth While Building a 7-Figure Business," my heart swells with pride and admiration. Evan-Nicole, through her unwavering determination, resilience, and unwavering spirit, has not only achieved remarkable success in the business world but has also crafted a masterpiece that will inspire and empower countless individuals to step into their greatness.

As I reflect on my own journey as an author, having written books like "Parables of Success" and "Supersize Your Success," I see a striking parallel between my daughter's path and my own. We both share a deep-seated belief in the power of personal growth as the cornerstone of success. We both understand that the road to achieving one's dreams is paved with challenges, setbacks, and moments of self-doubt. However, it is precisely in these moments that our true potential is revealed.

As I witness my daughter's success, I am reminded of the concept of "victim consciousness" versus "victor consciousness," a theme I have explored extensively in my own writings. Evan-Nicole embodies the true essence of a victor. She has not allowed her circumstances or the challenges she has faced to define her. Instead, she has chosen to rise above them, embrace her power, and create a life of extraordinary success.

"A Million Dollar Affair" is not just a book about building a 7-figure business; it is a testament to the transformative power of personal growth. It is a beacon of hope for all those who dream of achieving their full potential and creating a life of abundance and fulfillment. Evan-Nicole, through her words, her actions, and her very existence, has demonstrated that anything is possible when we align our thoughts, beliefs, and actions with our aspirations.

I am incredibly proud to call my daughter an author, an entrepreneur, and a victor. She is an inspiration to me, to her family, and to all those who have the privilege of knowing her. With "A Million Dollar Affair," she has not only written a book but also ignited a movement, empowering individuals worldwide to embrace their inner victor and create lives of extraordinary success.

—Jonathan ("Dad") Williams

www.ingramcontent.com/pod-product-compliance
Lightning Source LLC
Chambersburg PA
CBHW061245230426

43662CB00020B/2433